The Childhood of Jesus

Scripture text from
The Contemporary English Version

AMERICAN
BIBLE
SOCIETY

CHAPTER 1

Mary Expects a Baby

Emil Nolde
(1867-1956)
*White Amaryllis
with Mary and baby Jesus*

The artist paints the great
white flower towering over
Mary and her baby. What do
you think he is trying to show?

© Staatliche Graphische Sammlungen, Munich (Germany).

About 6 B.C.*

Countryside around Nazareth in Israel

At this time in the history of Israel, the Romans occupied the land and many other surrounding countries. The capital city was Jerusalem. About 70 miles to the north, among the hills of Galilee, was Nazareth, a small village with about 150 inhabitants. People from neighboring villages looked down on the Nazarenes, saying "Can anything good come from Nazareth?"

Mary, who later became the mother of Jesus, lived in this village. Like most young girls she was already promised to be married. Her husband-to-be was Joseph, a local carpenter. After the official ceremony, Mary would stay with her parents for a year and then go to live with her husband. Mary was expecting a baby.

* About 6 B.C.
It seems strange to say that Jesus was born in the years we identify as B.C. (before Christ). The six-year difference between his birth and the beginning of the period A.D. is due to a monk from Rome, Denis, who established our calendar in the sixth century, and was mistaken by about six years in his calculations of the year of Jesus' birth.

** About 80 years later
When Luke wrote, the time difference between the events he talked about and his writing about them was the same as if we were to tell the story of the First World War (1914 -1918).

About 80 Years Later

It was probably about 80 years later that Luke wrote his Gospel.**

Mary was no longer alive, but Luke may have known her well. She was a faithful "servant of the Lord."

For Luke and his fellow Christians, Jesus spoke for God in a new and different way. Luke began his Gospel by retelling an event that became known as the Annunciation, an event that clearly showed that Jesus was the true Son of God.

Craftsman making a door in a small Israeli village

3

The Annunciation

Luke 1.26-38

One month later God sent the angel Gabriel to the town of Nazareth in Galilee with a message for a virgin named Mary. She was engaged to Joseph from the family of King David. The angel greeted Mary and said, "You are truly blessed! The Lord is with you."

Mary was confused by the angel's words and wondered what they meant. When the angel told Mary, "Don't be afraid! God is pleased with you, and you will have a son. His name will be Jesus. He will be great and will be called the Son of God Most High. The Lord God will make him king, as his ancestor David was. He will rule the people of Israel forever, and his kingdom will never end."

Mary asked the angel, "How can this happen? I am not married!"

The angel answered, "The Holy Spirit will come down to you, and God's power will come over you. So your child will be called the holy Son of God. Your relative Elizabeth is also going to have a son, even though she is old. No one thought she could ever have a baby, but in three months she will have a son. Nothing is impossible for God!"

Mary said, "I am the Lord's servant. Let it happen as you have said." And the angel left her.

Angels

In the Bible, angels are messengers sent from God to give a message to humans; they are God's own messengers. An angel in a Bible story is a sign that God's will is being made known to humans.

David

David is considered Israel's greatest king. He was born in Bethlehem and ruled Israel for forty years, from about 1010 to 970 B.C. The memory of David remained alive among the people of Israel and they hoped for a kingdom that would be ruled by someone just like David. During the Roman occupation many people announced that Jesus was the "Son of David."

Holy Spirit

In the Bible the Holy Spirit creates and gives life. God's Spirit was present at creation (Genesis 1.2) and when Jesus was conceived (Luke 1.35). The Spirit is sometimes spoken of as "breath" or "wind."

Belonging to a Family

Birth

I exist, thanks to my parents' love. They have brought me into the world.

The same love

God's love is revealed in the parental love and in my birth. God's love is as boundless and tender as the love a mother and father have for their child.

A surname

When I was born, I received a last name from my parents. With this name I become a member of the family of those born with the same name.

A Christian name

My Christian name distinguishes me from those who have the same last name. People call me by my Christian name. My Christian name is me!

Baptism

Christians are baptised with the sign of water and the words "I baptize you in the name of the Father, and of the Son, and of the Holy Spirit." Christians believe that through baptism they join the family of the Church and all those who bear the name of the Son of God – Christ, from whom the name "Christian" comes.

One and Only

All, all, all:
the great and small,
humble and powerful,
sick and healthy,
rich and poor:

All, all, all:
white and yellow,
black and red,
wherever they come from,
the color of their skin
their origin:

God says to each one:
"My beloved child!"

To God each human being
is as precious
as an only child.
God cherishes each one
as a longed-for,
long-awaited child.
And to each
and to all
God entrusts a unique role,
a one and only place
in the world's story.

CHAPTER 2

A Child Is Born

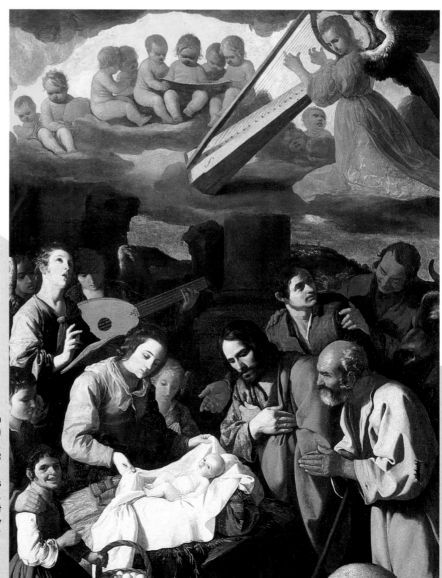

Francisco de Zurbaran
(1598-1664)
The Adoration of the Shepherds,
1638

Look carefully at the faces
of the people in the painting.
How does the artist show that
earth and heaven share the joy
of Jesus' birth?

© Photography Museum of Grenoble, Grenoble (France)

Born in a Stable

An inn in the desert, east of Jerusalem, where caravans and travelers can find lodging

Bethlehem was well known as the hometown of King David. In his time the people of Israel were free, but only a thousand years later, during the time of Mary and Joseph, the country was controlled by the Romans. In order to keep control of the collection of taxes, the Emperor Caesar Augustus (27 B.C. - A.D. 14) ordered a nationwide census to be taken.

Joseph and Mary went to Bethlehem to register with hundreds of other people, but they were unable to find anywhere to stay because of the crowds. They eventually had to spend the night in a stable where animals were kept. It was here that Jesus was born.*

The Story of Jesus' Birth

On special occasions we take photos: to help us remember a baby's first smile or the first steps. In Jesus' day there were no pictures, no records, no birth certificates with the date and place of birth.

When Luke was writing about Jesus' birth he did not have any written documents. But he may have used Mary's treasured memories of the event. Inspired by these he tells a wonderful story of angels, a wondrous light, and thunderous songs of glory. Luke was not writing a detailed record of Jesus' birth. He wants to draw us into the tremendous story of Jesus.

Statue of the Emperor Augustus Caesar, on the Capitoline Hill in Rome, Italy

* On what date was Jesus born?
No one knows for sure what month and day Jesus was born. But by the end of the fourth century Christians were celebrating the birth of Jesus on December 25th. Perhaps they chose it because many people recognized a festival on that exact day celebrating the "victorious sun." For Christians, Jesus was the radiant sun lighting up the world.

9

Christmas Night

Luke 2.1-14

About that time Emperor Augustus gave orders for the names of all the people to be listed in record books. These first records were made when Quirinius was governor of Syria.

Everyone had to go to their own hometown to be listed. So Joseph had to leave Nazareth in Galilee and go to Bethlehem in Judea. Long ago Bethlehem had been King David's hometown, and Joseph went there because he was from David's family.

Mary was engaged to Joseph and traveled with him to Bethlehem. She was soon going to have a baby, and while they were there, she gave birth to her first-born son. She dressed him in baby clothes and laid him on a bed of hay, because there was no room for them in the inn.

That night in the fields near Bethlehem some shepherds were guarding their sheep. All at once an angel came down to them from the Lord, and the brightness of the Lord's glory flashed around them. The shepherds were frightened. But the angel said, "Don't be afraid! I have good news for you, which will make everyone happy. This very day in King David's hometown a Savior was born for you. He is Christ the Lord. You will know who he is, because you will find him dressed in baby clothes and lying on a bed of hay."

Suddenly many other angels came down from heaven and joined in praising God. They said:
"Praise God in heaven!
Peace on earth to everyone
who pleases God."

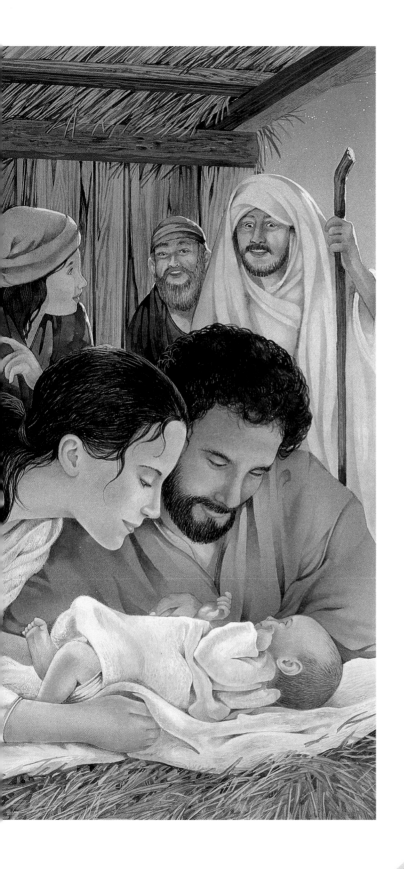

Christmas

The word comes from the old English *"Christes Maesse"* which means Mass of Christ. Today it is used for the celebration of Jesus' birth.

Shepherds

To those who believe that God speaks first to the mighty and the wealthy, Luke shows that God gives a special place to the despised, the poor, and the outcast; these were considered unimportant in the eyes of society, like the shepherds of Bethlehem.

Christ

The people of the Bible expected a Savior promised by God. This was to be the Messiah (the Hebrew word) or the Christ (the Greek word). The first Christians recognized Jesus as the promised Christ.

All Are Important

A Manger

Jesus is born in a manger, not a palace, not in gold or silk but in a poor place and wrapped in ordinary baby clothes.

The Shepherds

In Jesus' day, shepherds were people who didn't count and were usually despised because they were dirty and smelled of sheep; yet, they are the first to see and worship the baby Jesus born in the dirty manger.

The Unimportant

The shepherds represent the "little ones," the "unimportant," the "poor" and the "deprived" of all times.

The Favored

Many people in the world lack food, love, freedom, homes, and care. Perhaps because they have nothing and are waiting to be saved, God puts them first.

The Great Joy

God becomes a child, a human being on earth.
This is the great Christmas joy. God comes to share our life.
God becomes one of us.

Son of God

How astounding!
How amazing
to be born in a stable
and cradled in a manger
when this is he
the Almighty One,
the Son of God, who comes.

People expect of God
riches and power:
the Christmas story overturns that!

Jesus, the Son of God,
is born of a human mother
to become the brother
of every mother's child.

For when the Son of God
joins the human family
what can it mean
except that we are called
to be the children of God?

The Magi
from the East

Albrecht Dürer
(1471-1528)
Adoration of the Magi

Here is an artist who uses
detail to help us enjoy his
work. What do you learn
about the magi from
his painting?

© Alinari - Giraudon / Uffizi Gallery, Florence, Italy

After the Birth of Jesus

This mosaic, showing the Magi offering gifts to the child Jesus, was made in the sixth century after Christ. It can be seen in the church of St. Apollinarius in Ravenna, Italy

At the time of Jesus' birth, Herod the Great had been king of Judea for more than thirty years. He was a foreigner and became king with the support of the Roman Empire. Herod was hated, but he ruled through fear. His police were everywhere, most likely because he was afraid of losing his throne. Five days before his death, he even had one of his own sons executed! Matthew's Gospel remembers the murder of innocent children that had been ordered by Herod after he had heard about the birth of Jesus (Matthew 2.16-18).

When Matthew Wrote His Gospel

Matthew's Gospel was probably written more than eighty years after Herod's death. It was originally written for Christians of Jewish origin, or "Jewish-Christians." As they met together, people of other religions and other countries began to join them. Many of these were foreigners and strangers who were made welcome. Matthew shows in his Gospel that when Jesus was born, strangers – the Magi* – were also led to him.

The earliest Christians were often persecuted by the Romans. By recalling the bloodthirsty, cruel figure of Herod, Matthew showed Christians that persecution was also a part of Jesus' life from the very beginning.

Sunset over Bethlehem area in Israel

* Who were the Magi?
The "Magi" were astrologers from Babylon, Arabia or Persia. In these countries it was commonly believed that the birth of a famous person would be announced by the appearance of a star. It could be that Magi from the East had heard from Jews living among them that they were longing for a king sent by God.

The Magi

Matthew 2.1-12

When Jesus was born in the village of Bethlehem in Judea, Herod was king. During this time some wise men from the east came to Jerusalem and said, "Where is the child born to be king of the Jews? We saw his star in the east and have come to worship him."

When King Herod heard about this, he was worried, and so was everyone else in Jerusalem. Herod brought together the chief priests and the teachers of the Law of Moses and asked them, "Where will the Messiah be born?"

They told him, "He will be born in Bethlehem, just as the prophet wrote,
'Bethlehem in the land of Judea,
　you are very important among the towns of Judea.
From your town will come a leader,
　who will be like a shepherd for my people Israel.'"

Herod secretly called in the wise men and asked them when they had first seen the star. He told them, "Go to Bethlehem and search carefully for the child. As soon as you find him, let me know. I want to go and worship him too."

The wise men listened to what the king said and then left. And the star they had seen in the east went on ahead of them until it stopped over the place where the child was. They were thrilled and excited to see the star.

When the men went into the house and saw the child with Mary, his mother, they knelt down and worshiped him. They took out their gifts of gold, frankincense, and myrrh and gave them to him. Later they were warned in a dream not to return to Herod, and they went back home by another road.

The Star

The star guides the Magi to Jesus just as the angels showed the shepherds the way to Jesus in Luke's account.

Gifts

The Magi offer gold for a king, incense for a God, and myrrh (a resin used for perfume) for a human being. The Magi are wealthy, and Jesus came for the wealthy as well as the poor.

The Epiphany

The visit of the Magi is celebrated on the feast of the Epiphany on January 6th. *"Epiphany"* means God being shown, or revealed to the nations.

Searchers

Watchful

The Magi are "searchers," or "explorers" looking for God. Their minds and hearts are watchful, open to anything that might speak to them of God.

Signs

Those who search for God look for signs of God's presence.

Where are these signs?

They are found where people work toward friendship and solidarity, where people act out of a feeling of genuine love.

Strangers

The Magi are not from Bethlehem or even Palestine. They are strangers from a distant land.

Different

The Magi speak a foreign language, they have different customs, a different way of life, different clothing, a different religion. The Magi are different.

The Whole World

The many differences represented by the Magi show that the child of the manger is born not just for his own people, but for the whole world.

Always Pilgrims

How can we know God?
How can we find God?
How can we believe in God?

To come to God
and believe in God
we must undertake,
just as the Magi did,
a pilgrim journey,
a long search.

God does not force us to believe.
God invites us to a journey
of many meetings,
laying a pathway of signs
as mysterious and clear as the stars
in the sky.

At the crib everyone is welcome:
shepherds and strangers,
the poor and the rich,
people of different races and status.

For God there are no strangers:
all peoples are God's children;
all are embraced in the
same boundless love.

The world can only flourish
and grow better
if the differences
between peoples
become treasures
instead of barriers.

The Early Years

Frederico Barocci
(1535-1612)
The Circumcision

For a Jewish family, this is a solemn and joyful moment. The rich colors suggest this mood. What else does the Italian artist do to show that this is a special event?

© Photo R.M.N., Louvre Museum, Paris (France)

Life in Nazareth

Market Street in Nazareth, Israel

Jesus spent most of his life in Nazareth. He probably spoke Aramaic with a local accent. Among his first words would have been "immah" (mommy) and "abbah" (daddy). Jesus would have been taught the sacred language of the Jews, Hebrew, and he may have picked up some of the Greek and Latin used by soldiers, traders, and officials.

Jesus lived in a village. He would have watched his mother drawing water from the well, preparing yeast for baking bread, and seasoning food with salt. He would have seen his father working as a craftsman, a carpenter. He would have watched shepherds at the head of their flocks, the sower scattering seed and the vine-grower pruning vines on the hillside. He played with friends and grew up with them. Later they would find it difficult to remember Jesus as different. For them he remained "the carpenter's son."

Jesus was a Jew, and like every Jewish boy he was circumcised on the eighth day after his birth. His religious education started at home. On the Sabbath he would have gone to the synagogue with Joseph and heard about the Book of the Law, the first five books of our Bible. All through the year, the Jewish feasts* would have helped him to celebrate the story of the Jewish people.

Jewish man praying in Jerusalem, surrounded by the books of the Law

Hebrew writing

The Silence of the Gospels

The Gospels say very little about Jesus' life while growing up in Nazareth. This is because they are not intended to be a biography of Jesus. They are interested in his public life and message. What little they do say shows that Jesus' work in the world was built on this early life when he grew in wisdom and maturity.

* The Jewish feasts
The New Year feast recalls the Creation and the Passover, that is, the deliverance of the Hebrew people from Egypt. The Jewish feast of Pentecost is a reminder of the gift of the commandments given to Moses on Mount Sinai. And the Feast of Tabernacles or Booths commemorates the journey through the desert from Egypt to the Promised Land.

Growing up

Luke 2.21-40

Eight days later Jesus' parents did for him what the Law of Moses commands. And they named him Jesus, just as the angel had told Mary when he promised she would have a baby.

The time came for Mary and Joseph to do what the Law of Moses says a mother is supposed to do after her baby is born.

They took Jesus to the temple in Jerusalem and presented him to the Lord, just as the Law of the Lord says, "Each first-born baby boy belongs to the Lord." The Law of the Lord also says that parents have to offer a sacrifice, giving at least a pair of doves or two young pigeons. So that is what Mary and Joseph did.

At this time a man named Simeon was living in Jerusalem. Simeon was a good man. He loved God and was waiting for God to save the people of Israel. God's Spirit came to him and told him that he would not die until he had seen Christ the Lord.

When Mary and Joseph brought Jesus to the temple to do what the Law of Moses says should be done for a new baby, the Spirit told Simeon to go into the temple. Simeon took the baby Jesus in his arms and praised God,

"Lord, I am your servant,
and now I can die in peace,
because you have kept your promise to me.
With my own eyes I have seen
what you have done to save your people,
and foreign nations will also see this.
Your mighty power is a light for all nations,
and it will bring honor to your people Israel."

Jesus' parents were surprised at what Simeon had said. Then he blessed them and told Mary, "This child of yours will cause many people in Israel to fall and others to stand. The child will be like a warning sign. Many people will reject him, and you, Mary, will suffer as though you had been stabbed by a dagger. But all this will show what people are really thinking."

The prophet Anna was also there in the temple. She was the daughter of Phanuel from the tribe of Asher, and she was very old. In her youth she had been married for seven years, but her husband died. And now she was eighty-four years old. Night and day she served God in the temple by praying and often going without eating.

At that time Anna came in and praised God. She spoke about the child Jesus to everyone who hoped for Jerusalem to be set free.

After Joseph and Mary had done everything that the Law of the Lord commands, they returned home to Nazareth in Galilee. The child Jesus grew. He became strong and wise, and God blessed him.

Jesus

The name Jesus means "God saves." "Joshua" is Hebrew for Jesus. It was a common name among Jewish people in honor of Joshua who led the Israelites into the Promised Land. People did not have last names, and so Jesus would have been known as "Jesus, son of Joseph."

Circumcision

Circumcision is the removal of the male's foreskin. It is an ancient religious rite for Jewish people and is a sign of the covenant between God and Israel.

A Pair of Doves

The law prescribed two types of sacrifice. Rich people would offer a lamb, while poor people offered a pair of doves. Mary and Joseph were poor.

Discovery

A Baby

Jesus was a baby like any other baby: crying, laughing, sleeping, dreaming. He needed to be taken care of, to be fed, comforted, changed, cradled, and hugged.

The Customs of His People

Jesus was born into a particular people. He was educated according to the customs of his people and learned their way of life.

Learning

Every child needs to be helped and guided through the first steps of life, to learn the words of a language, to distinguish colors and objects.

Discovering

For a little child every day, every place is a novelty. People, objects, sounds, light and dark — these cause a child's eyes to widen, excited by each new discovery.

The Experience of Life

Tasting water, touching soil, falling on the ground, the first cut on a scraped knee, smiling, hugging, discovering his limits, learning obedience… Jesus has to experience life for himself.

Like Everybody!

Parents, family and friends,
and many others are needed
to help a child take those first
steps in life.

Is it possible to know God,
to learn to pray and worship
without the help of others?

Many stories have been made up
about Jesus the boy,
some saying he didn't find it
difficult to learn because
he knew it all already!

Jesus was a little child
like any other child
from anywhere.

Jesus knew the same joys,
the same difficulties,
the same struggles we know.

This is precisely why the Son
of God has come among us:
to live like everybody else!

CHAPTER 5

Adolescence

Hieronimus Bosch
(about 1450-1516)
Jesus among the Teachers

This artist has pictured the Jewish teachers in a setting that looks like his own Dutch homeland. Jesus is listening attentively. Can you see Joseph and Mary out in the street searching for him?

© Photo R.M.N. - Jean, Louvre Museum, Paris (France).

Jesus Is Twelve Years Old

Scale model of the city of Jerusalem

Going to Jerusalem was an extraordinary adventure for a twelve-year-old from a little village in the north of the country. Jerusalem was the capital, the Holy City. Jesus went with Mary and Joseph for the feast of the Passover. He would have walked across the countryside with the crowds of people going to Jerusalem, making friends, entering the city crowded with pilgrims, and finally seeing the Temple.* There he would have joined in the week of festivities.

Learned teachers taught and answered questions under the porches of the Temple. Many pilgrims, young and old, would stop to listen to the teachers. Even though he was only twelve, Jesus joined one of the groups and spoke with the teachers, forgetting all about Mary and Joseph.

When Luke Wrote His Gospel

One of the gates of the Old City of Jerusalem

Jesus lived in Nazareth for about thirty years, and Luke tells us about the only event mentioned from those years, the journey to Jerusalem. When Luke wrote his Gospel, the Temple might already have been in ruins (it was destroyed by the Romans in A.D. 70). But the teachers of the Law were still teaching and Luke wanted his readers to know that from the beginning the teaching of Jesus was more astounding than that of the scholars in the Temple.

Luke's readers found it difficult to understand who Jesus really was and who his father was. In this story Luke shows them that others found that difficult, too. Even Mary and Joseph did not fully understand who Jesus was.

* The Temple
Jerusalem's Temple was the most important religious place for the Jewish people. A large square was surrounded with colonnades and a central building was divided into three main areas: the outer courtyard, the Holy Place (sanctuary) and the Most Holy Place (symbolizing the presence of God).

27

B i b l e

Jesus among the Teachers

Luke 2.41-52

Every year Jesus' parents went to Jerusalem for Passover. And when Jesus was twelve years old, they all went there as usual for the celebration. After Passover his parents left, but they did not know that Jesus had stayed on in the city. They thought he was traveling with some other people, and they went a whole day before they started looking for him. When they could not find him with their relatives and friends, they went back to Jerusalem and started looking for him there.

Three days later they found Jesus sitting in the temple, listening to the teachers and asking them questions. Everyone who heard him was surprised at how much he knew and at the answers he gave.

When his parents found him, they were amazed. His mother said, "Son, why have you done this to us? Your father and I have been very worried, and we have been searching for you!"

Jesus answered, "Why did you have to look for me? Didn't you know that I would be in my Father's house?" But they did not understand what he meant.

Jesus went back to Nazareth with his parents and obeyed them. His mother kept on thinking about all that had happened.

Jesus became wise, and he grew strong. God was pleased with him and so were the people.

Passover

This feast celebrated the deliverance of the Israelites from slavery in Egypt.

Father

There are two meanings of the word "father" in this story. Can you find them?

Teachers

This does not mean school teachers, but experts in the Law of Moses (the Torah) who would explain it to believers.

Growing Up

Childhood

A child is taken by the hand. Children cannot decide everything for themselves. Grownups do this for them and teach them to do it for themselves. A child must be guided to learn.

Adolescence

The adolescent wants to choose his or her own way of life. Why should grown-ups be the only ones to give and refuse permission? The time will come when everyone must make his or her own choices and decisions.

Talking

Jesus participates in the adults' discussions. To the teachers of the Law, Jesus, a boy of twelve, also has something to say about knowing and loving God.

The Little Ones

Grown-ups don't know everything! Children and adolescents also have something to say about how they see God, life, love, and the world.

Choosing

Jesus decides to stay at the Temple. He makes his own choice. He thinks this is where he must be to show his true love for his Father.

Growing

Growing is not just about
getting stronger and bigger.

Growing is about becoming
capable of talking, thinking
and making decisions alone.

Growing is about becoming
capable of listening carefully,
accepting advice, weighing up
the pros and cons,
having the courage to accept the
consequences of difficult choices.

Growing is about learning to love
and give the best of ourselves,
and not, like a child,
getting everything just for our own
pleasure...

Growing is difficult.
It is a long process,
a never-ending task...

It has nothing to do with age.

Growing is about learning to trust
in order to become
somebody who is trustworthy.

Growing means searching
for God and continuing
to trust God
wholeheartedly.

The Feast of Christmas

Christmas is the feast of the birth of Jesus, the Son of God, at Bethlehem in Judea. No other feast is celebrated so much throughout the world. How has this come about? What are some Christmas customs?

The Date of Christmas

Nobody knows the exact day on which Jesus was born. From about the fourth century A.D. Christians were celebrating the birth of Jesus on December 25th. It's the time of the winter solstice when the sun's light becomes clear and warm again, and the days get longer. Christians wanted to make it clear that Jesus is the light of the world, bringing happiness to the whole human race.

Noel: *Dies Natalis*

Sometimes we sing carols about Christmas and use the word "Noel." The word comes from two Latin words, *dies natalis,* which mean "birthday." "Noel" is also connected with a French word which means "new" (nouvelle), showing that Jesus's birthday really is the Good News people had been waiting for.

The Crib

In 1223, Francis of Assisi made the first crib. It was in a cave in the little village of Greccio in Italy. He wanted to show the poverty into which Jesus was born.

Today, at Christmas time, the crib has a privileged place in homes and church. Whether made from gold or from clay, the crib recalls that Jesus, the Son of God, came to share the life of the poor and to uphold their dignity.

Advent

During the four weeks before December 25th Christians get ready for Christmas by reading the Bible, by praying and singing, by giving to the poor and helping the oppressed, and by decorating their houses. Some families make an Advent wreath by weaving small branches of evergreens together. They put four candles on it, one to be lit as each Sunday of Advent comes along in order to show that the light is getting brighter as Christmas approaches.

Ways of Celebrating Christmas

These days, Christmas is celebrated everywhere. Every country has its own special customs. From Lapland to Australia, from France to Russia, from Italy to Canada, you'll find the Christmas tree, the presents left by the chimney, the cakes and candies specially made for the feast, the candles left on the windowsills, the streets and houses lit up. All these ways of celebrating Christmas show that Jesus the Savior is the light coming to light up the world. They show, too, that he comes to bring every human person the gift of the love of God.

All these Christmas customs, no matter which country they are found in, have something in common:

- they express the joy of welcoming the Savior;
- they call us to share with the poor and needy;
- they proclaim that God came among us to help us to be happy;
- they sing out that Jesus the Savior brings dignity and freedom to those who have neither bread nor love.

Titles already published:

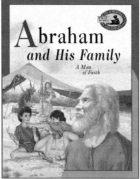

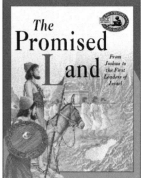

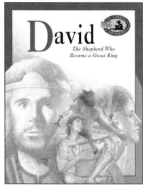

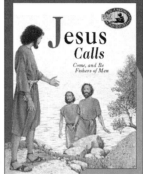

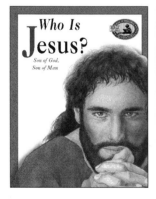

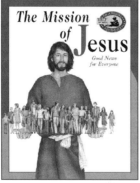

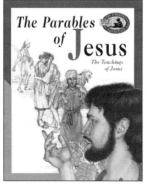

Forthcoming titles in the JUNIOR BIBLE Collection:

- The First Prophets
- Passion and Resurrection
- Exile and Return
- Isaiah, Micah, Jeremiah
- Jesus and the Outcasts
- Jesus in Jerusalem
- Acts
- Wisdom
- Psalms
- Women
- Revelation
- Letters

The Country of Jesus

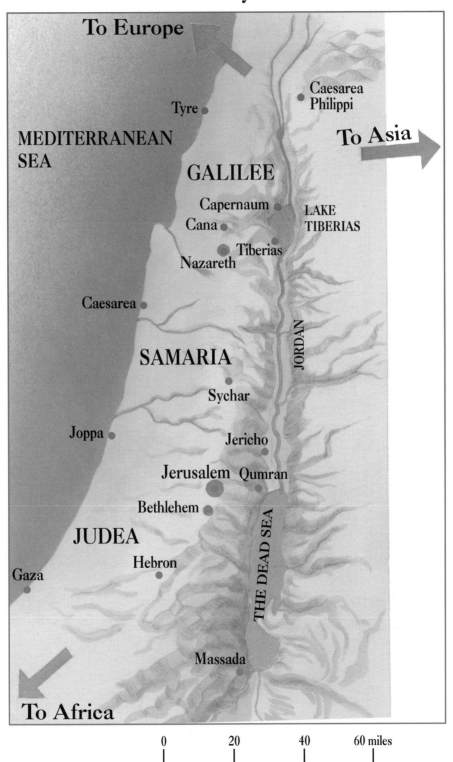

To Europe

Tyre

Caesarea
Philippi

MEDITERRANEAN
SEA

To Asia

GALILEE

Capernaum

Cana

LAKE
TIBERIAS

Nazareth

Tiberias

Caesarea

SAMARIA

JORDAN

Sychar

Joppa

Jericho

Jerusalem

Qumran

Bethlehem

JUDEA

Hebron

Gaza

THE DEAD SEA

Massada

To Africa

0   20   40   60 miles

The Childhood
of Jesus

Vol. 7

This is a Portion of Holy Scripture in the *Contemporary English Version*. The American Bible Society is a not-for-profit organization which publishes the Scriptures without doctrinal note or comment. Since 1816, its single mission has been to make the Word of God easily available to people everywhere at the lowest possible cost and in the languages they understand best. Working toward this goal, the ABS is a member of the United Bible Societies, a worldwide effort that extends to more than 180 countries and territories. You are urged to read the Bible and to share it with others. For a catalog of other Scripture publications, call us toll-free at 1-800-32 BIBLE, or write to the American Bible Society, 1865 Broadway, New York, NY 10023. Visit our website: **www.americanbible.org**

© 1998 ÉDITIONS DU SIGNE

Original text by:	Liam KELLY, Anne WHITE, Albert HARI, Charles SINGER
English text adapted by:	The American Bible Society
Photography:	Frantisek ZVARDON
Illustrators:	Mariano VALSESIA, Betti FERRERO MIA. Milan Illustrations Agency
Layout:	Bayle Graphic Studio

ISBN 1-58516-135-7
Printed in Italy - Stige, Torino
Eng. Port. CEV 560 P - 109853
ABS 8-9/00